 First Edition. www.cjjvrei.com

Dedication

To my wife, **Sherry**—your unwavering love, patience, and belief in me have been the foundation beneath every deal, every risk, and every win. This journey wouldn't mean half as much without you by my side.

To my Facebook® group members—your encouragement, insights, and camaraderie have fueled my growth more than you know. You've helped turn ambition into action.

And to the following honorable mentions—mentors, leaders, and trailblazers who've inspired, guided, and supported me through the highs and lows of real estate investing:
Jesse R. Stanton (Growth Co.)
Matt Beard (No Fluff Real Estate)
Mike Turner (Mobile Home Investing Club)
Lee Arnold (Lee Arnold System of Real Estate Investing)
Stephanie Lombardo (Flippin'Launch)
Mitch Messer (UnFundableAF)
Blake Choisnet (Rentals2Wealth Community)
Tiffany & Josh High (Results Driven® Community)

Your wisdom, generosity, and example have helped me build not just a portfolio—but a purpose. This book is a tribute to the power of partnership, and I'm grateful to each of you for being part of mine.

Table Of Contents

Chapter 1: Introduction to Equity Partnerships in Property

Understanding Equity Partnerships

Equity partnerships in real estate provide a powerful strategy for investors looking to maximize their returns while minimizing risks. These partnerships allow individuals to pool resources, share knowledge, and leverage each other's strengths to acquire properties that may otherwise be out of reach. Investors can benefit from the combined financial power, which often leads to larger investments and more significant opportunities within the property market. Understanding the dynamics of equity partnerships is crucial for anyone looking to thrive in today's competitive landscape.

One of the primary advantages of equity partnerships is the ability to raise capital for real estate acquisitions. Traditional financing methods can be restrictive, particularly for first-time buyers or those looking to expand their portfolios. By forming partnerships, investors can access funds from multiple sources, including private equity and crowdfunding strategies. This collaborative approach not only eases the financial burden but also diversifies investment risks, making it an attractive option for many.

Moreover, being an equity partner in real estate allows investors to engage in joint ventures that can lead to lucrative opportunities. These partnerships often involve sharing responsibilities, from property management to decision-making, which can enhance the overall investment experience. Investors can learn from each other's expertise and navigate the complexities of the market more effectively. This shared approach can be particularly beneficial in identifying undervalued properties and executing successful fix-and-flip strategies.

Navigating the legal considerations in real estate partnerships is essential to ensure a smooth collaboration. Understanding the contractual obligations, profit-sharing agreements, and exit strategies are critical for all parties involved. It is advisable for investors to seek legal counsel when forming partnerships to avoid potential disputes and ensure compliance with local regulations. A well-structured partnership agreement can protect the interests of all parties and foster a successful long-term relationship.

Finally, equity partnerships also present unique tax strategies for real estate investors. By structuring investments in a way that maximizes tax benefits, investors can enhance their overall profitability. This may involve exploring various financing options or establishing a real estate investment fund that allows for more strategic capital growth. Investors must stay informed about current tax laws and regulations to take full advantage of the benefits available through equity partnerships. In this ever-evolving market, adaptability and knowledge are key to maximizing returns through collaboration.

Benefits of Collaboration in Real Estate

Collaboration in the real estate sector offers numerous advantages, particularly for investors, wholesalers, and those involved in fix-and-flip projects. By pooling resources, expertise, and networks, individuals can leverage each other's strengths, leading to better investment opportunities. This synergy not only enhances the potential for higher returns but also mitigates risks associated with real estate investments. When investors work together, they can tackle larger projects that may have been beyond their individual capacity.

One of the primary benefits of collaboration is the ability to raise capital more efficiently. When real estate investors unite, they can attract more significant investment sums, making it easier to fund acquisitions. This collective approach can also facilitate access to crowdfunding platforms and private equity, providing diverse financing options that may not be available to solo investors. As a result, partnerships enable investors to engage in more ambitious ventures, thereby increasing their overall market presence.

Joint ventures are particularly advantageous, allowing partners to share both the financial burden and the rewards of property investment. This arrangement provides a safety net; if a project encounters challenges, the impact is distributed among the partners rather than falling solely on one individual. Additionally, partners can combine their knowledge and expertise, leading to more informed decision-making and improved project outcomes. Such collaborations foster a learning environment where all parties can grow and enhance their investment strategies.

Tax strategies can also be optimized through collaboration, as partners can share insights on deductions and credits that may apply to their investments. By pooling their knowledge, investors can identify more efficient structures for their partnerships, ensuring compliance while maximizing tax benefits. This aspect of collaboration is particularly beneficial for those new to real estate, as experienced partners can guide them through complex regulations and financial considerations.

Finally, navigating the legal landscape of real estate partnerships can be daunting. Collaboration allows investors to pool their resources not just financially but also in legal expertise. By working together, partners can ensure that all legal considerations are addressed and that their agreements protect their interests. This collective approach to legal matters enhances trust and transparency, which are essential for successful long-term partnerships in the competitive real estate market.

Chapter 2: Raising Capital for Real Estate Acquisition

Traditional Financing Methods

Traditional financing methods have long been the backbone of real estate investment, providing a reliable means for investors to fund their projects. These methods include conventional loans, hard money lending, and personal savings. Each option comes with its own set of advantages and challenges, making it essential for investors to understand the nuances of these financing routes before embarking on their property ventures.

Conventional loans are often the first choice for many investors, as they typically offer lower interest rates and longer repayment terms compared to other financing methods. However, securing a conventional loan usually requires a strong credit history, a substantial down payment, and thorough documentation of income and assets. This can be a barrier for first-time buyers or those with less-than-perfect credit.

Hard money loans, on the other hand, provide a more flexible alternative for investors who may not qualify for traditional financing. These loans are often secured by the property itself and are typically offered by private lenders. While they come with higher interest rates and shorter repayment periods, they can be a valuable resource for fix-and-flip investors needing quick access to capital. The speed at which hard money lenders operate can be a significant advantage in competitive markets.

Personal savings represent another traditional financing avenue, enabling investors to leverage their own funds without incurring debt. This method allows for greater control over the investment process and can simplify transactions, as there are no lenders involved. However, relying solely on personal savings can limit the scope of investment opportunities, as investors may not have sufficient capital to pursue larger projects or diversify their portfolios.

Incorporating these traditional financing methods into a broader investment strategy can enhance an investor's ability to navigate the complexities of real estate partnerships and joint ventures. Understanding how each method works, as well as their respective advantages and limitations, is crucial for real estate investors aiming to maximize their returns and build a sustainable investment portfolio. Investors should carefully assess their financial situation and goals to determine which financing options align best with their overall strategy.

Alternative Funding Sources

In the realm of real estate investment, alternative funding sources have emerged as viable options for those looking to maximise their returns. Traditional financing methods, such as bank loans, may not always be accessible or suitable for every investor. Alternative funding sources, including private equity, crowdfunding, and joint venture partnerships, provide a diversified approach to raising capital. Understanding these options allows real estate investors, wholesalers, and fix-and-flippers to explore innovative avenues to fund their projects and achieve their investment goals.

Private equity is a significant player in alternative funding, offering investors the opportunity to pool resources for larger real estate ventures. This method not only provides the necessary capital but also brings in expertise and strategic guidance that can enhance project success. By partnering with private equity firms, real estate investors can leverage their networks and resources, creating a more robust investment strategy that aligns with their financial objectives. This collaborative approach can yield substantial returns when executed correctly.

Crowdfunding has revolutionized the way real estate projects are financed, making it accessible to a broader range of investors. Through online platforms, individuals can invest in real estate ventures with relatively small amounts of capital. This democratization of investment allows for shared risk and the potential for high returns. Real estate investors should consider integrating crowdfunding strategies into their funding mix, as it not only broadens their investor base but also fosters community engagement and support for their projects.

Joint venture partnerships represent another alternative funding source, where two or more parties collaborate to fund a real estate project. These partnerships can be particularly beneficial for first-time property buyers or those lacking sufficient capital. By pooling resources, partners can share the financial burden and risks associated with real estate investment. Moreover, joint ventures can provide access to valuable expertise, enhancing the overall project execution and increasing the likelihood of success.

Finally, understanding the legal considerations involved in alternative funding sources is crucial for real estate investors. Each funding method comes with its own set of regulations and legal frameworks that must be adhered to. Navigating these legalities not only protects investors but also ensures that partnerships are structured in a way that maximizes returns while minimizing risks. By being informed about the legal landscape, investors can confidently pursue alternative funding options and build successful real estate ventures.

Building a Network for Capital Raising

Building a network for capital raising is essential for real estate investors looking to enhance their opportunities and maximize returns. Establishing connections with other investors, lenders, and financial institutions can provide access to necessary funds, allowing for more significant investments and joint ventures. Networking not only opens doors for potential equity partnerships but also fosters a community where knowledge and expertise can be shared, benefiting all parties involved.

Engaging with local real estate investment groups, attending property expos, and joining online forums are effective strategies for expanding your network. These platforms allow you to meet like-minded individuals who are also interested in raising capital for property investments. By actively participating in these groups, you can build relationships that may lead to future collaborations and access to investment opportunities that may not be publicly advertised.

In addition to traditional networking, leveraging social media platforms such as LinkedIn can be a powerful tool for connecting with potential investors and partners. Sharing insights, success stories, and investment strategies through professional profiles can attract individuals interested in collaborating on real estate projects. Establishing a reputable online presence can significantly enhance your credibility, making it easier to raise capital when needed.

It's essential to remember that building a network is not just about seeking investment; it's also about offering value to others. Providing assistance, sharing knowledge, and being open to collaboration can create a mutually beneficial environment that encourages investment and partnership. This reciprocal approach fosters trust and strengthens relationships within your network, ultimately leading to more successful capital raising efforts.

Lastly, as you build your network, consider the importance of legal considerations. Understanding the regulatory framework governing partnerships and investments in real estate is crucial to avoid potential pitfalls. By being informed and compliant with legal requirements, you can secure the trust of your network, ensuring that your capital raising efforts are both effective and sustainable.

Chapter 3: Investing in Real Estate

Types of Real Estate Investments

Real estate investment encompasses various types, each offering unique opportunities and risks. Among the most common types are residential properties, which include single-family homes, condominiums, and multi-family units. Investors in this sector often seek to generate income through rental payments or benefit from property appreciation over time. Understanding the dynamics of the residential market is crucial for investors aiming to maximize their returns.

Commercial real estate is another lucrative investment avenue. This category includes office buildings, retail spaces, and industrial properties, which typically require a larger capital outlay but can yield higher returns. Investors may engage in long-term leases with businesses, providing a steady income stream. However, the commercial market can be volatile, influenced by economic factors such as employment rates and consumer spending.

Real estate investment trusts (REITs) represent a more accessible option for those looking to invest in property without direct ownership. REITs allow investors to buy shares in a company that owns or finances income-producing real estate. This investment vehicle offers the benefit of liquidity and diversification, allowing investors to spread their capital across various types of properties and geographic locations.

Crowdfunding platforms have emerged as a modern method for raising capital in real estate. This approach allows multiple investors to pool their resources to finance a property project. It not only democratizes access to real estate investments but also enables smaller investors to participate in larger ventures. However, thorough due diligence is essential, as the success of crowdfunding initiatives can vary significantly.

Lastly, joint ventures in property investment can provide a strategic partnership model for investors seeking to share risks and resources. By collaborating with other investors or firms, individuals can leverage each other's strengths and expertise, leading to more significant investment opportunities. This type of partnership can be particularly advantageous in navigating complex legal and financial considerations, making it an attractive option for both novice and seasoned investors.

Evaluating Investment Opportunities

Evaluating investment opportunities in real estate is a crucial step for any investor looking to maximize returns. Understanding the local market dynamics, including property values, demand, and economic indicators, can provide insights into potential investment success. Factors such as location, property type, and surrounding amenities play a significant role in determining the attractiveness of an investment. A thorough analysis of these elements can help investors make informed decisions that align with their financial goals.

One effective strategy for evaluating properties is the use of comparative market analysis (CMA). This involves examining similar properties in the area that have recently sold or are currently on the market. By assessing the sale prices and rental rates of comparable properties, investors can gauge whether a property is priced appropriately. Additionally, this analysis can uncover potential opportunities for value-add investments, such as renovations or repositioning, that can significantly enhance returns.

Investors should also consider the financial metrics associated with each opportunity. Key performance indicators such as cash flow, return on investment (ROI), and cap rates are essential in assessing the viability of a property. These metrics help investors understand not only the immediate financial implications but also the long-term appreciation potential. It's important to run various scenarios, including best and worst-case outcomes, to prepare for market fluctuations.

In the context of equity partnerships, evaluating investment opportunities also involves assessing the strengths and weaknesses of potential partners. Collaborative investments can leverage diverse expertise and resources, increasing the likelihood of a successful outcome. Establishing clear communication and alignment of goals with partners is crucial in navigating the complexities of joint ventures, ensuring that all parties are on the same page regarding expectations and responsibilities.

Finally, staying informed about legal considerations is paramount when evaluating investment opportunities. Investors must be aware of regulations governing property investments, including zoning laws, tax implications, and financing options. Engaging with legal professionals who specialize in real estate can provide essential guidance and help mitigate risks associated with non-compliance. By integrating these evaluations into their investment strategy, investors can enhance their chances of achieving sustainable success in the property market.

Risk Assessment in Property Investment

Risk assessment is a critical component of property investment, particularly for real estate investors, wholesalers, and fix and flippers. Understanding potential risks allows investors to make informed decisions and safeguard their investments. It involves identifying various factors that could affect the profitability of a property, including market trends, location, and property condition. By systematically evaluating these risks, investors can better position themselves for success in a competitive market.

One of the primary aspects of risk assessment is conducting thorough market research. This includes analyzing local market conditions, property demand, and economic indicators that can impact property values. Investors should consider the historical performance of the area and any upcoming developments that may influence growth. Additionally, understanding demographic shifts and buyer preferences can provide valuable insights into potential risks and opportunities in the property investment landscape.

Another critical element of risk assessment is evaluating the physical condition of a property. Investors must conduct detailed inspections to identify any structural issues, necessary repairs, or compliance with local regulations. This not only helps in estimating renovation costs but also aids in anticipating future expenses that could affect cash flow. A well-maintained property generally carries a lower risk profile, making this assessment vital for both immediate investments and long-term value preservation.

Financial risks also play a significant role in property investment. Investors must assess their financing options, including interest rates, loan terms, and the potential impact of market fluctuations on their investment returns. Understanding the intricacies of tax strategies and how they affect overall profitability is equally crucial. By being aware of potential financial pitfalls, investors can ensure they have adequate capital reserves and contingency plans in place to mitigate risks associated with unforeseen market changes or property issues.

Lastly, legal considerations should not be overlooked in the risk assessment process. Engaging with legal experts to navigate the complexities of property law, joint venture agreements, and equity partnerships can help investors avoid costly disputes and ensure compliance with regulations. By undertaking a comprehensive risk assessment that encompasses market analysis, property condition, financial implications, and legal factors, real estate investors can make strategic decisions that enhance their chances of success in equity partnerships and collaborative ventures.

Chapter 4: Being an Equity Partner in Real Estate

Roles and Responsibilities of Equity Partners

Equity partners play a crucial role in property investment by bringing together diverse skills, resources, and networks. Their primary responsibility is to contribute capital, which is essential for acquiring real estate assets. However, financial investment is just one aspect; equity partners must also engage in active decision-making regarding property management, development strategies, and exit plans. This collaboration ensures that all partners are aligned in their goals and maximizes the potential for returns on investment.

Structuring Equity Deals

Structuring equity deals in real estate requires a clear understanding of the various components involved. Investors must first identify the type of partnership they wish to pursue, whether it be a joint venture or a private equity arrangement. Each structure has its own set of advantages and disadvantages, which can significantly impact the returns on investment. By carefully assessing these options, stakeholders can align their goals and expectations, ultimately leading to a more successful collaboration.

Once the partnership type is established, the next step involves determining the equity contribution of each partner. This includes not only the initial capital investment but also the value of non-cash contributions, such as expertise, time, and resources. Clear agreements on these contributions are essential to avoid misunderstandings later in the partnership. Additionally, outlining the profit-sharing structure at this stage is crucial, as it sets the foundation for how returns will be distributed among partners based on their respective stakes.

Legal considerations play a significant role in structuring equity deals. Investors must ensure that all agreements comply with local laws and regulations to prevent future disputes. Consulting with legal professionals who specialize in real estate can help navigate these complexities. Furthermore, drafting a well-structured partnership agreement that addresses potential contingencies, exit strategies, and dispute resolution mechanisms is vital for safeguarding the interests of all parties involved.

Tax strategies also come into play when structuring equity deals. Investors should be aware of the tax implications associated with different partnership structures. For instance, joint ventures may offer unique tax benefits that can enhance overall returns. Therefore, it is advisable for partners to collaborate with tax advisors to optimize their financial positions and take full advantage of available deductions and credits.

Finally, as real estate markets evolve, so too must the strategies employed in structuring equity deals. Investors should remain flexible and open to innovative financing options, including crowdfunding and investment funds. By staying informed about market trends and emerging opportunities, equity partners can ensure that their investments not only meet current needs but also position them for future success in the dynamic landscape of real estate.

Effective Communication Among Partners

Effective communication among partners is fundamental in any equity partnership within the real estate sector. Clear and open lines of communication foster trust and understanding, which are essential for successful collaborations. Partners must ensure that they are aligned in their goals, expectations, and investment strategies, as miscommunication can lead to misunderstandings and conflicts that may jeopardize the partnership. Regular meetings and updates can help maintain transparency and keep all parties informed of progress and challenges.

In addition to regular communication, it is crucial for partners to establish formal channels for discussing important decisions. This structure can include scheduled conference calls, emails summarizing discussions, and shared platforms for project management. By documenting agreements and conversations, partners create a reference point that can help resolve disputes and clarify intentions. Effective communication also involves active listening, where each partner's opinions and concerns are valued and addressed, promoting a collaborative spirit.

The role of technology in enhancing communication cannot be overstated. Utilizing tools such as messaging apps, video conferencing platforms, and project management software can streamline interactions and ensure that partners remain connected regardless of their geographical locations. By embracing these technologies, partners can share documents, updates, and feedback in real-time, which is particularly beneficial in the fast-paced world of real estate investment.

Moreover, cultural differences among partners can impact communication styles and perceptions. It is important for partners from diverse backgrounds to be aware of these differences and to adapt their communication methods accordingly. Building cultural competence can lead to more effective interactions and help in negotiating deals that respect the values and practices of all involved. Partners should strive to create an inclusive environment where everyone feels comfortable expressing their views.

Finally, addressing communication issues promptly is vital for maintaining healthy partnerships. If misunderstandings arise, partners should seek to resolve them quickly through open dialogue. Ignoring communication breakdowns can lead to resentment and a decline in collaboration. By fostering an environment of honesty and accountability, partners can enhance their relationships and ultimately achieve better results in their real estate ventures.

Chapter 5: Crowdfunding Strategies for Real Estate Projects

Overview of Real Estate Crowdfunding

Real estate crowdfunding has emerged as a transformative method for raising capital in the property investment sector. It allows individual investors to pool their resources to finance larger projects that would otherwise be beyond their reach. This innovative approach not only democratizes access to real estate investment but also diversifies risk across multiple stakeholders, making it an attractive option for both seasoned investors and newcomers alike.

The process typically involves an online platform where project owners present their properties and investment opportunities to potential backers. Investors can browse various projects, assess potential returns, and choose how much to invest based on their financial capacity. This level of accessibility has opened doors for many who wish to enter the real estate market without the need for substantial upfront capital, thereby fostering a collaborative investment environment.

Crowdfunding strategies in real estate can vary widely, from equity crowdfunding to debt-based models. Equity crowdfunding allows investors to acquire ownership stakes in the property, sharing in the profits from rental income and eventual sales. Conversely, debt crowdfunding involves lending money in exchange for interest payments, offering a different risk-reward profile. Understanding these distinctions is crucial for investors looking to align their strategies with their financial goals and risk appetite.

Moreover, the legal landscape surrounding real estate crowdfunding is continually evolving. As regulatory frameworks adapt to accommodate this growing sector, investors must navigate various legal considerations to ensure compliance and protect their interests. This includes understanding the implications of securities regulations, tax obligations, and the rights and responsibilities inherent in joint venture partnerships.

In conclusion, real estate crowdfunding represents a significant opportunity for investors to engage in property ventures with reduced barriers to entry. By leveraging collective resources, investors can access larger and potentially more lucrative projects while diversifying their portfolios. As the market matures, staying informed about the latest trends, strategies, and legal requirements will be essential for maximizing returns and achieving long-term success in the real estate landscape.

Platforms for Crowdfunding Investments

In recent years, crowdfunding has emerged as a transformative platform for real estate investments, offering a unique alternative to traditional financing methods. This innovative approach allows investors to pool their resources, enabling them to participate in larger projects that may have previously been out of reach. Platforms such as RealtyMogul and Fundrise have gained popularity for their ability to connect individual investors with lucrative property deals, making it easier than ever to engage in equity partnerships.

The benefits of crowdfunding go beyond mere accessibility. By leveraging technology, these platforms provide detailed information on various investment opportunities, allowing investors to make informed decisions. Investors can review project specifics, including property valuations, projected returns, and the experience of the project sponsors. This level of transparency is crucial for building trust and ensuring that all partners are aligned in their investment goals.

Moreover, crowdfunding platforms often cater to a diverse range of investment strategies, accommodating both seasoned investors and novices. Whether one is looking to invest in residential properties, commercial developments, or even fix-and-flip projects, there are tailored options available. This flexibility not only diversifies an investor's portfolio but also helps mitigate risk through varied exposure across different sectors of the real estate market.

Legal considerations play a vital role in crowdfunding investments, and it is essential for investors to understand the regulatory landscape. Platforms must comply with securities laws and regulations, which can vary significantly from one jurisdiction to another. By ensuring that these platforms operate within legal frameworks, investors can protect their interests and minimize potential liabilities associated with crowdfunding ventures.

As the real estate market continues to evolve, embracing crowdfunding as a legitimate investment strategy presents an array of opportunities. Investors who recognize the potential of these platforms can enhance their ability to raise capital and engage in lucrative projects. By fostering collaboration through crowdfunding, real estate investors can build robust partnerships, ultimately maximizing returns and achieving collective success in their ventures.

Legal Considerations in Crowdfunding

Crowdfunding has emerged as a popular method for raising capital in the real estate sector, but it is imperative to understand the legal landscape that governs such funding mechanisms. Investors must comply with various regulations, particularly those outlined by the Securities and Exchange Commission (SEC) in the United States. These regulations dictate how securities can be offered and sold, which is crucial for ensuring that crowdfunding campaigns are legally compliant and protect both the investors and the project developers.

One key legal consideration is the classification of offerings under the SEC's guidelines. Depending on the amount of capital being raised, offerings may fall under different exemptions, such as Regulation D or Regulation A. These classifications affect the disclosure requirements and the types of investors that can participate in the crowdfunding campaign. Real estate investors must carefully navigate these regulations to avoid legal pitfalls that could jeopardize their projects or lead to severe penalties.

Additionally, agreements with investors should be meticulously drafted to outline the terms of the partnership. This includes specifying the rights and obligations of each party, how profits will be distributed, and what happens in the event of a dispute. Clear documentation not only fosters transparency but also shields investors from potential legal issues. It is advisable to engage legal counsel experienced in real estate and securities law to ensure that all agreements are robust and enforceable.

Tax implications also play a vital role in the legal considerations of crowdfunding. Investors should be aware of how their participation in a crowdfunding venture may affect their tax liabilities. Factors such as income recognition, capital gains, and deductions can significantly impact the financial returns from their investments. Understanding these tax strategies is essential for maximizing the benefits of equity partnerships in real estate.

Finally, staying informed about changes in legislation is crucial for anyone involved in real estate crowdfunding. Laws and regulations can evolve, and what is compliant today may not be tomorrow. Regularly consulting with legal experts and industry professionals can help investors stay ahead of the curve and make informed decisions that safeguard their investments and partnerships. Keeping abreast of legal developments not only ensures compliance but also enhances the overall success of real estate crowdfunding initiatives.

Chapter 6: Private Equity in Real Estate Ventures

Understanding Private Equity Structures

Private equity structures play a pivotal role in the realm of real estate investing. These structures are designed to pool capital from various investors, allowing them to collectively invest in larger properties or projects than they could on their own. Understanding how these structures function is essential for real estate investors, wholesalers, and fix and flippers who wish to maximize their returns through collaboration and strategic partnerships.

One of the most common private equity structures is the limited partnership. In this arrangement, there are general partners who manage the investment and limited partners who provide the capital but have no say in the daily operations. This structure offers a balance between control and investment, giving active investors the ability to direct the project while allowing passive investors to benefit from their expertise without being involved in the management.

Crowdfunding has emerged as a modern method of raising capital for real estate ventures, evolving from traditional private equity models. Platforms that facilitate real estate crowdfunding allow multiple investors to contribute smaller amounts towards a specific project, democratizing access to real estate investments. This approach not only diversifies risk but also opens up opportunities for smaller investors who may not have the capital to enter the market independently.

Tax strategies are another critical consideration within private equity structures. Investors must be aware of the various tax implications associated with different structures, such as limited liability companies or real estate investment trusts. Properly navigating these tax considerations can significantly impact overall returns, making it essential for investors to seek professional advice and optimize their tax positions when engaging in private equity investments.

Finally, joint venture partnerships are a popular choice for real estate investors looking to pool resources and expertise. By collaborating with other investors or firms, parties can share risks and benefits while undertaking more substantial projects. Understanding the nuances of these partnerships, including legal considerations and profit-sharing arrangements, is crucial for anyone looking to thrive in the competitive real estate market.

Benefits and Drawbacks of Private Equity

Private equity in real estate offers a unique avenue for investors to maximize their returns through strategic partnerships. One of the primary benefits is the access to substantial capital, which allows for larger acquisitions and developments that individual investors may not be able to undertake alone. This pooling of resources can lead to enhanced purchasing power and the ability to leverage opportunities in the market that require significant financial backing. Furthermore, private equity firms often bring expertise in management and operational efficiencies, which can greatly improve the performance of a property investment.

However, investing in private equity also comes with its drawbacks. Investors typically face higher fees compared to traditional investment routes, which can eat into potential profits. Additionally, private equity investments often require a longer-term commitment, locking investors in for several years before they can realize returns. This lack of liquidity can be a significant concern for those who prefer more immediate access to their funds, especially in a fluctuating market.

Another crucial aspect to consider is the level of control investors have when entering a private equity arrangement. While some investors appreciate the hands-off approach, others may find it challenging to relinquish decision-making authority regarding their investments. This dynamic can lead to tension between equity partners, especially if the goals and strategies of the involved parties are not aligned from the outset.

Tax strategies also play a pivotal role in the decision to engage in private equity ventures. Investors must be well-versed in the tax implications associated with their contributions and potential returns. Certain structures can provide tax advantages, such as depreciation benefits, but these often require careful planning and professional advice to optimize. Understanding these financial nuances is essential for investors looking to maximize their overall returns and ensure compliance with tax regulations.

Finally, the legal considerations involved in private equity partnerships must not be overlooked. Drafting comprehensive agreements that outline the roles, responsibilities, and expectations of all parties is critical to avoid disputes down the line. Investors should seek legal counsel to navigate these complexities effectively, ensuring that their interests are protected and that they are fully aware of their rights and obligations within the partnership. This careful approach can help foster a collaborative environment, ultimately leading to the success of the investment venture.

Case Studies of Successful Private Equity Deals

In recent years, the private equity sector has witnessed several notable successes in real estate investments, demonstrating the potential of well-structured deals. One case study that stands out involves a private equity firm that acquired a portfolio of distressed commercial properties in a major city. By implementing a robust turnaround strategy, including renovations and enhanced property management, the firm was able to increase the value of the properties significantly, resulting in impressive returns for its investors. This case exemplifies the importance of identifying undervalued assets and having a clear vision for their revitalization.

Another successful deal involved a joint venture partnership between a private equity firm and a local developer to construct a mixed-use development in an emerging market. The collaboration allowed the private equity firm to leverage the developer's local expertise while providing the necessary capital for the project. The result was a thriving community space that attracted both residents and businesses, ultimately yielding substantial profits for both parties. This case highlights the effectiveness of strategic partnerships in maximizing investment outcomes.

In the realm of crowdfunding, a private equity firm successfully raised capital through an online platform to finance a residential development project. By marketing the opportunity to a diverse pool of investors, they not only secured the necessary funds but also engaged a community of stakeholders who became passionate advocates for the project. This approach not only provided financial backing but also built a network of support that enhanced the project's visibility and success, showcasing the power of modern fundraising strategies in real estate.

Moreover, a private equity deal involving the acquisition of a struggling hotel chain illustrates the potential of repositioning assets. The firm recognized the value in rebranding and repositioning the properties to cater to a different market segment. By investing in renovations and updating marketing strategies, the hotel chain transformed into a profitable venture, demonstrating how creative thinking and effective management can lead to successful outcomes in real estate investments.

Lastly, a case study focusing on tax strategies for private equity investors highlights the importance of understanding legal frameworks. A firm that capitalized on specific tax incentives available for real estate investments was able to maximize returns for its investors while minimizing their tax liabilities. This case serves as a reminder that knowledge of legal considerations can enhance the profitability of equity partnerships in property, making it essential for investors to stay informed and strategically navigate the complexities of the real estate market.

Chapter 7: Tax Strategies for Real Estate Investors

Understanding Property Tax Implications

Understanding property tax implications is crucial for real estate investors, wholesalers, and fix-and-flippers alike. Property taxes can significantly impact the overall profitability of a venture, and being aware of these implications can guide investment strategies. Investors must consider local tax laws, as they can vary widely from one jurisdiction to another, affecting not only the costs but also the potential returns on investment.

One key aspect to understand is how property taxes are assessed. Local governments typically calculate taxes based on the assessed value of a property, which may differ from its market value. Investors should be proactive in understanding the assessment process and keep abreast of any changes that could lead to increased tax liabilities. Additionally, knowing how to appeal assessments can sometimes lead to lower property taxes, thus enhancing the cash flow of an investment.

Investors should also consider the timing of property taxes. Some jurisdictions impose taxes based on the calendar year, while others may have different fiscal periods. Understanding when taxes are due and how they can affect cash flow is essential for effective financial planning. For instance, new investors must factor in these expenses when raising capital for acquisitions or structuring joint venture partnerships.

Moreover, the implications of property taxes extend beyond acquisition; they also influence resale strategies. Investors who plan to fix and flip properties should factor in potential tax liabilities when determining their selling price. This is particularly important in markets where property values are increasing, as rising taxes can erode profits if not anticipated correctly.

Finally, leveraging tax strategies can provide significant advantages in property investments. Knowledge of tax deductions, credits, and incentives available for real estate investments can enhance returns. Investors should consult with tax professionals to ensure they are maximizing their benefits, particularly when engaging in equity partnerships or crowdfunding strategies for real estate projects. Understanding these nuances allows investors to navigate the complexities of property taxes while optimizing their investment outcomes.

Tax Deductions and Benefits

Tax deductions and benefits play a crucial role in enhancing the financial viability of real estate investments. For investors, understanding which expenses are deductible can significantly affect their overall profitability. Common deductions include mortgage interest, property taxes, and operational expenses, which help in reducing the taxable income from rental properties. By taking full advantage of these deductions, investors can strategize their financial position to maximize returns on their investments.

In addition to standard deductions, real estate investors should be aware of various tax benefits available specifically for property transactions. For instance, the capital gains tax exemption on the sale of a primary residence can provide substantial savings. Furthermore, 1031 exchanges allow investors to defer paying capital gains taxes when they reinvest the proceeds from a sold property into another similar property. This strategy is particularly beneficial for those looking to grow their investment portfolio without incurring significant tax liabilities.

Equity partnerships in property investment also offer unique tax advantages. When forming joint ventures, partners can pool their resources and share both the risks and rewards of property investments. The profits generated from these partnerships can be distributed in a manner that optimizes each partner's tax situation. By structuring the partnership carefully, investors can benefit from lower tax rates on capital gains and potentially access tax credits available for specific real estate developments.

Crowdfunding strategies have gained popularity in recent years, and understanding the tax implications of these investments is essential for real estate investors. Each investment made through a crowdfunding platform may come with its own set of tax considerations. Investors should consult with tax professionals to navigate these complexities effectively, ensuring that they can maximize their returns while remaining compliant with tax regulations.

Ultimately, tax strategies for real estate investors must be integrated into their overall investment plans. By staying informed about changes in tax legislation and leveraging available deductions and benefits, investors can make informed decisions that enhance their financial outcomes. Collaborating with tax advisors and financial professionals is advisable to create a tailored approach that aligns with individual investment goals and maximizes the potential benefits of property ownership.

Long-Term Tax Planning Strategies

Long-term tax planning strategies are essential for real estate investors looking to maximize their returns while minimizing their tax liabilities. By understanding the various tax implications of property investments, investors can make informed decisions that enhance their financial outcomes. These strategies often involve a combination of proactive planning, leveraging tax deductions, and utilizing investment vehicles that offer favorable tax treatment. A well-structured approach can lead to significant savings over time and contribute to the overall success of investment ventures.

One effective strategy is to take advantage of tax deferral options available through specific investment structures. For instance, using a self-directed IRA or a 1031 exchange allows investors to defer taxes on gains when reinvesting in similar properties. This deferral can significantly boost an investor's purchasing power, allowing them to acquire more assets without the immediate burden of tax payments. Moreover, understanding the nuances of these options is crucial, as they can vary based on individual circumstances and the type of properties involved.

In addition to deferral strategies, investors should also focus on maximizing deductions related to their real estate activities. Common deductions include mortgage interest, property taxes, and operating expenses such as repairs and maintenance. However, it is important to keep meticulous records to substantiate these deductions during tax season. Engaging a tax professional with expertise in real estate can provide valuable insights and ensure that all eligible deductions are claimed, optimizing the investor's tax position.

Another long-term strategy involves the formation of partnerships or joint ventures. By pooling resources with other investors, individuals can leverage collective buying power and share the tax benefits associated with property investments. Equity partnerships can also facilitate access to more significant investment opportunities, as well as spread the risk among partners. Structuring these partnerships correctly can lead to favorable tax treatment, making them an attractive option for serious investors looking to scale their portfolios.

Finally, staying informed about changes in tax legislation is crucial for long-term tax planning. Tax laws can evolve, and new opportunities or constraints may arise that impact real estate investment strategies. Regularly consulting with tax professionals and participating in educational workshops can help investors remain compliant while taking advantage of any new incentives. By being proactive in their tax planning, real estate investors can ensure that their financial strategies align with current regulations, ultimately protecting and enhancing their investment returns.

Chapter 8: Joint Venture Partnerships in Property Investment

Defining Joint Ventures in Real Estate

Joint ventures in real estate represent a strategic alliance between two or more parties who come together to achieve a specific investment goal. These partnerships are particularly beneficial in the property market, where the financial and operational demands can be significant. By pooling resources, expertise, and capital, joint ventures allow investors to leverage their strengths while mitigating risks associated with real estate investments. Understanding the structure and purpose of joint ventures is crucial for investors looking to maximize their returns in this competitive sector.

The formation of a joint venture typically involves a legal agreement that outlines the roles, responsibilities, and contributions of each partner. This agreement serves as a blueprint for the partnership, defining how profits and losses will be shared, decision-making processes, and exit strategies. Investors must carefully consider these elements to ensure alignment of interests and avoid potential conflicts. It is essential that all parties are transparent about their expectations and capabilities, fostering a collaborative environment that is conducive to success.

One significant advantage of joint ventures is the ability to raise capital more effectively. By combining financial resources, partners can undertake larger projects that may have been unattainable individually. This aspect is particularly relevant in the current market, where rising property prices and competition necessitate innovative funding strategies. Investors can explore various financing options through joint ventures, including private equity and crowdfunding, which can enhance their investment capabilities and lead to greater profitability.

Moreover, joint ventures can provide access to specialized knowledge and networks that individual investors may lack. Each partner brings unique skills and insights, whether in property management, market analysis, or legal considerations. This collective expertise can result in more informed decision-making and ultimately lead to better investment outcomes. As the real estate landscape evolves, leveraging partnerships becomes increasingly important for navigating challenges and seizing opportunities.

In conclusion, joint ventures in real estate are a powerful tool for investors seeking to enhance their portfolios. By understanding the intricacies of these partnerships, including their structure, benefits, and potential pitfalls, investors can position themselves for success. Collaboration through joint ventures not only enables access to greater capital and expertise but also fosters a sense of community among real estate professionals. As the industry continues to grow, embracing this collaborative approach will be key to maximizing returns.

Structuring Joint Ventures for Success

Structuring a joint venture in real estate requires careful planning and alignment of interests among all parties involved. Investors must first identify their objectives and ensure that these align with potential partners. This includes understanding the financial goals, risk tolerance, and desired level of involvement in the project. A clear articulation of these elements lays the groundwork for a successful partnership, fostering trust and transparency right from the outset.

Next, the legal framework of the joint venture must be established. This involves drafting detailed agreements that outline the roles, responsibilities, and profit-sharing mechanisms for each partner. Legal considerations are crucial, as they protect all parties and clarify expectations. Investors should work closely with legal professionals who specialize in real estate to ensure that all agreements are comprehensive and enforceable, minimizing the risk of disputes down the line.

Financial structuring is another key component of successful joint ventures. Investors must determine how capital will be raised and allocated within the partnership. This may involve contributions from each partner, securing external financing, or utilizing crowdfunding strategies. A well-defined financial structure not only enhances the project's viability but also reassures investors about the management of their funds, which is essential for fostering confidence and commitment to the partnership.

Communication is vital throughout the duration of the joint venture. Regular updates and meetings should be scheduled to discuss project progress, address concerns, and make necessary adjustments. Establishing open lines of communication helps to mitigate misunderstandings and keeps all partners engaged. This collaborative approach can lead to innovative solutions and improved outcomes, ultimately maximizing returns for everyone involved.

Finally, evaluating the performance of the joint venture upon completion is crucial for future success. Investors should analyze both financial results and the overall partnership experience to identify lessons learned. This evaluation not only informs future joint ventures but also enhances the skills and strategies of each partner, contributing to their growth and success in the competitive real estate market.

Navigating Challenges in Joint Ventures

Joint ventures in real estate offer exciting opportunities, but they are not without their challenges. Investors must navigate the complexities of aligning goals with their partners, which can often lead to friction if expectations are not clearly defined from the outset. Establishing a solid foundation built on mutual trust and transparency is crucial for the success of any joint venture. Without this, even the most promising projects can become mired in disputes that derail progress and erode relationships.

One common challenge in joint ventures is the disparity in investment philosophies and risk appetites among partners. Investors may have different views on how much capital to allocate, the types of properties to invest in, or the timeline for returns. This divergence can lead to disagreements, making it essential for partners to engage in open dialogue and clearly document their respective roles and contributions. A well-structured partnership agreement can serve as a guide to mitigate these tensions and ensure everyone is on the same page.

Navigating legal considerations is another significant aspect of joint ventures. Investors must be aware of the legal implications of their agreements, including profit-sharing arrangements, liability issues, and exit strategies. It is advisable to seek legal counsel familiar with real estate partnerships to draft comprehensive agreements that protect all parties involved. This diligence can prevent costly misunderstandings and provide a framework for resolving disputes should they arise.

Moreover, securing financing can present challenges, particularly if partners have differing credit profiles or financial capabilities. Joint ventures require a cohesive approach to raising capital, which can involve crowdfunding strategies or private equity investments. Investors must work collaboratively to present a unified front to potential lenders or investors, showcasing the strengths of their combined resources and expertise to improve their chances of securing favorable financing terms.

Finally, ongoing communication is vital as the project progresses. Regular check-ins can help partners stay aligned on their goals and address any emerging issues before they escalate. Creating a culture of accountability and openness fosters a more resilient partnership, allowing investors to navigate the inevitable challenges of joint ventures with confidence. By maintaining a proactive approach, partners can maximize their chances of success and achieve their investment objectives together.

Chapter 9: Financing Options for First-Time Property Buyers

Understanding Mortgage Basics

Understanding the basics of mortgages is essential for real estate investors, wholesalers, and fix and flippers. A mortgage is essentially a loan secured by real property, allowing individuals to purchase homes or investment properties without needing the full purchase price upfront. By grasping how mortgages work, investors can better strategize their property acquisitions and maximize their returns. This foundational knowledge also aids in making informed decisions when entering equity partnerships or crowdfunding ventures in real estate.

There are various types of mortgages available, each with its own terms and conditions. Fixed-rate mortgages, for instance, offer stability with consistent monthly payments, whereas adjustable-rate mortgages can fluctuate, potentially leading to lower initial payments but greater long-term costs. Understanding these options is crucial for investors, particularly those who are new to the market, as it influences their cash flow and overall investment strategy. Additionally, being aware of the current interest rates can help you seize opportunities in the market more effectively.

The process of obtaining a mortgage involves several steps, including pre-approval, application, and closing. Pre-approval gives investors a clearer understanding of their budget and strengthens their position when negotiating with sellers. During the application process, lenders assess the borrower's creditworthiness, which can significantly impact the terms of the mortgage. A strong credit score can lead to more favorable interest rates, making it essential for investors to maintain good financial health.

Real estate investors must also consider the importance of down payments when securing a mortgage. A larger down payment can reduce monthly payments and possibly eliminate the need for private mortgage insurance (PMI). This factor is particularly relevant in joint venture partnerships, where multiple investors may pool resources to manage the down payment and financing aspects of a property acquisition. Understanding how to leverage down payments effectively can enhance the potential returns of an investment.

Lastly, it is crucial for investors to navigate the legal considerations involved in mortgages. This includes understanding the terms of the mortgage agreement and the implications of defaulting on a loan. Investors should also be aware of potential tax advantages related to mortgage interest deductions. This knowledge not only assists in protecting investments but also allows for strategic planning in equity partnerships and real estate ventures, ensuring all parties are aligned and informed throughout the process.

Government Schemes for First-Time Buyers

Government schemes for first-time buyers play a crucial role in easing the pathway to property ownership, particularly for those navigating the complexities of real estate investment. These initiatives are designed to provide financial assistance and incentives, making the dream of owning a home more attainable. For investors, understanding these schemes can not only create opportunities for collaboration but also enhance their strategy in raising capital for real estate acquisitions.

One of the most prominent schemes available is the Help to Buy programs, which offers equity loans to first-time buyers. This initiative allows buyers to purchase a new-build home with just a 5% deposit, while the government provides an equity loan of up to 20% of the property's value. For real estate investors involved in joint venture partnerships, this could present potential opportunities to work with first-time buyers, ensuring a mutually beneficial arrangement that can lead to profitable outcomes.

Additionally, the First Homes scheme aims to provide discounted homes to local first-time buyers, offering properties at a significant reduction to market prices. This scheme not only supports buyers but also fosters community growth and stability. Real estate wholesalers and fix-and-flip investors might find that engaging with these buyers can lead to quicker sales and higher demand for properties that meet the criteria of these government-backed initiatives.

Moreover, tax reliefs and incentives are often tied to these schemes, further enhancing their attractiveness. For example, first-time buyers may benefit from exemptions on stamp duty, which can substantially reduce the overall cost of purchasing a property. By understanding these financial implications, equity partners in real estate ventures can better navigate legal considerations and structure their deals to maximize returns.

Finally, the importance of education and awareness cannot be overstated. Real estate investors should familiarize themselves with the various schemes available and how they evolve over time. Attending workshops or seminars on government initiatives can provide valuable insights and networking opportunities, helping investors to stay ahead of the curve and leverage these resources effectively in their property investment strategies.

Alternative Financing Solutions

In the realm of real estate investment, traditional financing routes may not always be the most viable option. Alternative financing solutions have emerged as effective methods for securing capital, particularly for investors seeking to maximize their returns through collaboration. These alternatives not only provide flexibility but also open doors to different types of investment opportunities that may otherwise be inaccessible through conventional means. Real estate investors, wholesalers, and fix and flippers can benefit significantly from understanding and utilizing these financing options.

One of the most popular alternative financing solutions is crowdfunding. This method allows multiple investors to pool their resources together to fund real estate projects. Crowdfunding platforms have made it easier for both seasoned and novice investors to participate in larger deals that were once limited to institutional investors. By leveraging the power of the crowd, investors can diversify their portfolios and reduce risks associated with single property investments.

Private equity is another avenue worth exploring for those looking to enhance their real estate ventures. Private equity firms typically invest in real estate projects in exchange for equity stakes, offering investors access to substantial capital without the burden of traditional loans. This approach can help streamline the financing process and provide a more efficient way to fund larger projects, whether it be residential complexes or commercial properties.

Joint venture partnerships also present a robust alternative for financing real estate acquisitions. By teaming up with other investors, individuals can share resources, expertise, and risks associated with property investments. This collaborative approach not only enables participants to pool their capital but also allows them to leverage each partner's strengths in navigating the complexities of real estate transactions. Such arrangements can lead to more successful outcomes and higher returns.

Finally, understanding the legal considerations involved in alternative financing is essential for any investor. Establishing clear agreements and understanding the terms of investment can prevent disputes and ensure that all parties are aligned in their goals. Real estate investors should take the time to consult with legal professionals to navigate these complexities, ensuring that their partnerships are not only profitable but also compliant with applicable laws and regulations.

Chapter 10: Building a Real Estate Investment Fund

Fundamentals of Real Estate Investment Funds

Real estate investment funds serve as a pivotal mechanism for investors looking to pool resources and maximize their returns in the property market. These funds allow individuals and institutions to collaborate, sharing both the risks and rewards associated with property investments. By participating in a fund, investors gain access to a diversified portfolio of real estate assets, which can mitigate the risks typically associated with direct property ownership. This approach is particularly beneficial for those who may lack the capital or expertise to invest in real estate independently.

One of the key advantages of real estate investment funds is the ability to leverage collective capital for larger projects. This is especially important in the current market, where high-value properties often require substantial financial backing. By pooling resources, investors can engage in joint ventures that would be unattainable individually, thus increasing their potential for higher returns. Fund managers play a crucial role in this process, providing expertise in property selection, management, and exit strategies, which can significantly enhance the investment experience.

Raising capital for real estate acquisition through investment funds also opens up avenues for innovative financing strategies. For instance, crowdfunding has emerged as a popular method for attracting small-scale investors to larger projects. This democratization of property investment allows individuals to participate in lucrative opportunities that were once reserved for wealthy investors or institutional players. As such, understanding the mechanics of crowdfunding and the legal implications surrounding it becomes essential for anyone looking to establish a successful investment fund.

Moreover, the legal considerations surrounding real estate partnerships and investment funds cannot be overlooked. Investors must navigate a complex landscape of regulations, ensuring compliance with securities laws and fund management practices. It is vital for fund managers and investors to have a clear understanding of their rights, responsibilities, and potential liabilities. Engaging with legal professionals who specialize in real estate can provide invaluable guidance, helping to safeguard investments and facilitate smoother operations within the fund.

In summary, the fundamentals of real estate investment funds revolve around collaboration, strategic capital raising, and adherence to legal frameworks. By understanding these elements, investors can optimize their participation in equity partnerships and enhance their overall investment strategy. Whether you are a seasoned investor or new to the market, grasping these core principles will enable you to navigate the dynamic landscape of real estate investment effectively.

Steps to Establishing a Fund

Establishing a fund for real estate investment is a strategic approach that can significantly enhance your ability to acquire properties and maximize returns. The first step involves defining the fund's purpose and investment strategy. This includes determining the type of properties you wish to invest in, whether residential, commercial, or mixed-use. A clear understanding of your investment goals will guide your decisions and attract the right investors who share your vision.

Next, it is essential to assemble a capable team that can help navigate the complexities of real estate investment. This team should include legal advisors, accountants, and experienced real estate professionals. Their expertise will be invaluable in structuring the fund, ensuring compliance with regulations, and optimizing tax strategies. A well-rounded team enhances credibility and can attract more capital from potential investors.

Once the team is in place, the next step is to create a detailed business plan for your fund. This plan should outline your investment thesis, target market, and financial projections. Including strategies for risk management and exit strategies will further strengthen your proposal. A comprehensive business plan not only serves as a roadmap for your fund but also as a persuasive document to attract investors.

After solidifying your business plan, the focus shifts to raising capital. This can be achieved through various methods, such as private equity, crowdfunding, or joint venture partnerships. Each method has its own advantages and challenges; therefore, it is crucial to choose the one that aligns with your fund's goals and structure. Engaging in networking and marketing efforts can also help reach a broader audience of potential investors.

Finally, establishing a legal framework for your fund is critical. This involves drafting and filing necessary legal documents, including the fund's operating agreement and subscription agreements. Understanding and navigating the legal considerations in real estate partnerships will protect both your interests and those of your investors. Ensuring transparency and good governance will foster trust and encourage ongoing investment in your fund.

Attracting Investors to Your Fund

Attracting investors to your fund is a crucial step in the journey of real estate investment. A well-structured fund can offer potential investors a clear understanding of the value proposition and the lucrative opportunities available in the real estate market. Start by defining your investment strategy and articulate how it aligns with the current market trends. This clarity will not only attract interest but also help in building trust among potential investors.

Chapter 11: Navigating Legal Considerations in Real Estate Partnerships

Essential Legal Documents for Partnerships

In the realm of equity partnerships within real estate, having the right legal documents is paramount to ensuring a smooth operation and protecting the interests of all parties involved. A partnership agreement serves as the cornerstone of any collaborative venture, outlining the roles, responsibilities, and contributions of each partner. This document should detail how profits and losses will be shared, decision-making processes, and mechanisms for resolving disputes, thereby establishing a clear framework for the partnership's functioning.

Another essential document is the operating agreement, particularly for limited liability companies (LLCs). This agreement delineates the governance structure of the LLC, specifying how the business will be managed and how decisions will be made. It also typically includes provisions for adding new partners, transferring ownership interests, and addressing the dissolution of the partnership, which are critical for future growth and potential changes in the partnership dynamics.

Confidentiality agreements are also crucial, especially when dealing with sensitive information related to investments, strategies, or financial details. These documents protect the proprietary information of each partner and ensure that any shared knowledge does not lead to competitive disadvantages or breaches of trust. By formalizing confidentiality expectations, partners can engage more freely in discussions and negotiations, knowing their information is safeguarded.

Moreover, investors should consider implementing buy-sell agreements, which outline the process for a partner wishing to exit the partnership. Such agreements can prevent misunderstandings and conflicts by establishing a predetermined method for valuing the partnership interest and facilitating a smooth transition. This foresight is particularly important in the volatile real estate market, where circumstances can change rapidly.

Finally, legal compliance cannot be overlooked. It is essential for partners to ensure that all documents comply with local laws and regulations governing real estate transactions. Engaging with a legal professional who specializes in real estate partnerships can help navigate these complexities, ensuring that all necessary documents are in place and correctly executed. This diligence not only protects individual interests but also enhances the overall credibility and success of the partnership.

Compliance with Real Estate Laws

In the realm of real estate investment, compliance with applicable laws is crucial for ensuring the sustainability and success of any venture. Investors, wholesalers, and flippers must be well-versed in local, state, and federal regulations that govern property transactions. This compliance not only protects investors from legal repercussions but also enhances their reputation in the market, making it easier to forge partnerships and secure funding. Understanding the legal landscape allows investors to navigate challenges effectively while maximizing their returns through strategic collaborations.

Real estate laws encompass a wide range of areas including zoning, property rights, and environmental regulations. Investors should be aware of zoning laws that dictate how properties can be used, as these laws can significantly impact property value and investment potential. Additionally, understanding property rights is essential, particularly when engaging in equity partnerships or joint ventures. Investors need to ensure that all parties involved have clear and legal rights to the properties in question to avoid disputes that could derail a project.

Furthermore, tax strategies play a pivotal role in compliance, as they can directly affect an investor's bottom line. Real estate investors must be knowledgeable about tax obligations, including property taxes and potential deductions related to investment expenses. Collaborating with tax professionals can provide investors with insights into how to structure their investments in a tax-efficient manner, ultimately increasing their overall return on investment. This proactive approach to tax compliance not only aids in maximizing profits but also minimizes the risk of audits or legal issues.

Crowdfunding and private equity ventures are increasingly popular in real estate, but they come with their own set of legal considerations. Investors looking to raise capital through these means must comply with securities laws that govern fundraising activities. This includes understanding the requirements for disclosures and investor qualifications. Ensuring compliance in these areas is essential to avoid penalties and to maintain the integrity of the investment, fostering trust among potential investors and partners.

In conclusion, compliance with real estate laws is not merely a legal obligation but a strategic advantage for investors. By prioritizing legal considerations, investors can safeguard their ventures against potential pitfalls and create a solid foundation for growth. Educating oneself about the intricacies of real estate law, tax strategies, and funding regulations is essential for anyone looking to thrive in the competitive field of property investment. Through diligence and collaboration, real estate investors can navigate the complexities of compliance effectively, paving the way for successful and profitable partnerships.

Dispute Resolution Mechanisms

Dispute resolution mechanisms are essential in the realm of equity partnerships, particularly in property investment. For real estate investors, wholesalers, and fix-and-flippers, having a clear understanding of these mechanisms can prevent conflicts from escalating and safeguard investments. Common methods include negotiation, mediation, and arbitration, each offering varying levels of formality and involvement. Understanding these options allows parties to choose the most appropriate path based on the nature of their dispute and the relationship between the partners involved.

Negotiation is often the first step in resolving disputes, allowing parties to communicate directly and seek a mutually beneficial solution. This informal approach can save time and costs associated with more formal mechanisms. When partners have built a strong relationship, they may find that open dialogue can resolve misunderstandings before they escalate into significant issues. Investors should cultivate negotiation skills as part of their overall strategy to enhance collaboration and minimize potential friction.

If negotiation fails to yield a satisfactory resolution, mediation can be a valuable next step. In this process, a neutral third party facilitates discussions between the disputing parties, helping them to identify their interests and explore possible solutions. Mediation is particularly effective in real estate partnerships where maintaining ongoing relationships is crucial. This method can often lead to creative solutions that satisfy both parties, thus preserving the partnership and the investment.

Arbitration is a more formal dispute resolution mechanism and is often seen as a hybrid between mediation and litigation. In arbitration, a neutral arbitrator makes a binding decision based on the evidence and arguments presented by both parties. This method can be beneficial for real estate investors seeking a definitive resolution when negotiations and mediation have failed. However, parties must consider the potential costs and time involved, as arbitration can be more expensive than other forms of dispute resolution.

Ultimately, the choice of dispute resolution mechanism will depend on the specific circumstances and the preferences of the parties involved. It is crucial for real estate investors to incorporate dispute resolution strategies into their partnership agreements. By doing so, they can ensure that they are prepared to handle any disagreements that may arise, thereby protecting their investments and maximizing returns through effective collaboration.

Chapter 12: Conclusion: The Future of Equity Partnerships in Property

Trends in Real Estate Investment

The landscape of real estate investment is constantly evolving, driven by shifts in market dynamics, technology, and investor preferences. In recent years, there has been a marked increase in interest towards collaborative investment models, such as equity partnerships and joint ventures. These arrangements allow investors to pool resources, share risks, and leverage diverse expertise, ultimately leading to enhanced returns. As real estate investors, wholesalers, and fix and flippers look to maximize their opportunities, understanding these trends is crucial for staying competitive in the market.

Crowdfunding has emerged as a significant trend in real estate investment, providing new avenues for raising capital. This strategy allows multiple investors to contribute small amounts of money towards larger projects, democratizing access to real estate ventures. For those within the niche of private equity, this shift signifies a move towards more inclusive investment structures, where even smaller investors can participate in lucrative opportunities. Understanding the mechanics of crowdfunding platforms and their regulatory requirements is essential for investors aiming to capitalize on this trend.

Tax strategies also play a pivotal role in shaping real estate investment trends. Investors are increasingly seeking ways to optimize their tax liabilities through strategic planning, such as utilizing 1031 exchanges or investing in opportunity zones. These strategies not only enhance cash flow but also encourage reinvestment in the property market. For real estate investors and equity partners, being knowledgeable about these tax implications can significantly influence their investment decisions and overall profitability.

Joint venture partnerships are gaining traction as a preferred method for financing real estate projects. By collaborating with other investors or firms, individuals can leverage combined resources and expertise to tackle larger and more complex projects. This trend highlights the importance of building strong networks and establishing trust among partners, as successful collaborations often hinge on shared goals and aligned interests. For wholesalers and fix and flippers, understanding the dynamics of joint ventures can open doors to previously inaccessible markets and projects.

As the real estate investment landscape continues to change, staying informed about these trends is vital. Investors must adapt by embracing technology, understanding new financing options, and developing strategic partnerships. By doing so, they can navigate the complexities of the market effectively, ensuring sustained growth and profitability in their real estate ventures. Keeping a pulse on these trends will not only enhance investment strategies but also foster long-term relationships that are essential in this collaborative environment.

The Importance of Adaptability in Partnerships

In the fast-paced world of real estate, adaptability has emerged as a crucial trait for successful partnerships. Investors, wholesalers, and fix and flippers must recognise that the property market is not static; it is influenced by economic shifts, changing regulations, and evolving consumer preferences. Those who can adjust their strategies and expectations in response to these factors are more likely to thrive. Being open to new ideas, flexible in decision-making, and willing to pivot when necessary can significantly enhance the effectiveness of partnerships in property investment.

When forming equity partnerships, it is essential to establish a clear understanding of each partner's strengths and weaknesses. Adaptability allows partners to leverage their unique skills and experiences, fostering a collaborative environment. For example, a partner with expertise in raising capital can work alongside a partner skilled in market analysis to create a comprehensive investment strategy. This synergy not only maximises returns but also mitigates risks, as partners can shift roles and responsibilities based on the current market landscape.

Crowdfunding has transformed the way real estate investors secure funding, and adaptability is vital in this arena. Investors must be prepared to adjust their approaches to attract diverse investors who may have varying expectations and preferences. By being receptive to feedback and embracing innovative funding solutions, partners can enhance their appeal in a competitive marketplace. This flexibility not only aids in raising capital but also strengthens relationships with investors, ensuring sustained support for future projects.

Legal considerations in real estate partnerships can also demand a high level of adaptability. As regulations change, partners must be willing to reassess their agreements and strategies to remain compliant. This might involve renegotiating terms, adjusting profit-sharing models, or even restructuring the partnership itself. By maintaining a proactive stance and being open to change, partners can avoid potential pitfalls and ensure that their collaborations remain fruitful and legally sound.

Ultimately, the importance of adaptability in partnerships cannot be overstated. As real estate investors navigate the complexities of the market, those who embrace change and remain versatile will find themselves better positioned for success. Whether through joint ventures, private equity, or investment funds, an adaptable mindset will empower partners to seize opportunities and overcome challenges, leading to maximized returns and sustained growth in their real estate ventures.

Final Thoughts on Maximizing Returns Through Collaboration

In the world of real estate investing, the power of collaboration cannot be overstated. By forming equity partnerships, investors can pool resources, share expertise, and ultimately enhance their potential returns. This collective approach allows for a diversification of risk, making it an attractive strategy for those looking to maximise their investments. The synergy created through collaboration can lead to more informed decision-making and access to opportunities that might otherwise be out of reach.

Engaging in joint ventures or crowdfunding can provide investors with the chance to tap into larger projects that require more capital than they might possess individually. This not only enables participation in lucrative deals but also fosters a community of like-minded individuals who can support one another. By leveraging each partner's strengths, such as capital, knowledge, or networks, the group can navigate the complexities of real estate transactions more effectively.

Tax strategies are another critical component when considering equity partnerships in property. Collaborative investments can often lead to more favourable tax outcomes, as partners can share deductions and take advantage of tax breaks that may not be available to solo investors. Understanding these implications can significantly influence the overall profitability of a project, making it essential for partners to engage in thorough financial planning and consultation.

Moreover, the legal considerations surrounding real estate partnerships cannot be overlooked. Establishing clear agreements and understanding each partner's rights and responsibilities is vital to maintaining a harmonious working relationship. By addressing potential legal pitfalls upfront, collaborators can avoid disputes that could derail investment goals and affect returns. This proactive approach not only enhances trust among partners but also solidifies the foundation for future ventures.

In conclusion, maximising returns through collaboration in real estate is not just a strategy; it is a necessity in today's competitive market. By embracing equity partnerships, investors can unlock new levels of success while mitigating risks. The journey to financial growth and stability is often smoother when shared, and those who leverage the power of collaboration will likely find themselves at the forefront of the real estate landscape, poised to seize opportunities as they arise.

Equity (n)...

The ownership stake that turns your money into muscle. It's not just a slice of the pie—it's the power to profit from appreciation, cash flow, and control. Equity means your capital works for you, building wealth while others handle the grind. It's the silent engine behind every smart deal, and the key to turning partnerships into profit. In real estate, equity isn't just value—it's leverage. And when you team up with the right people, it's your ticket to passive income, legacy wealth, and financial freedom.

www.ingramcontent.com/pod-product-compliance
Lightning Source LLC
LaVergne TN
LVHW022304200926
848481LV00004B/1211
* 9 7 9 8 2 3 1 6 5 3 3 5 5 *